Contents

1. Places

Day 1

A Words to Know

Highlight the words you know.

Target Words

bank	cafeteria	coffee shop	post office
park	hospital	pharmacy	playground
hotel	bakery	bus stop	supermarket
library	theater	bookstore	amusement park
museum	restaurant	department store	
school	hair salon	convenience store	

B Town Map

Find your way around the town. Look and write.

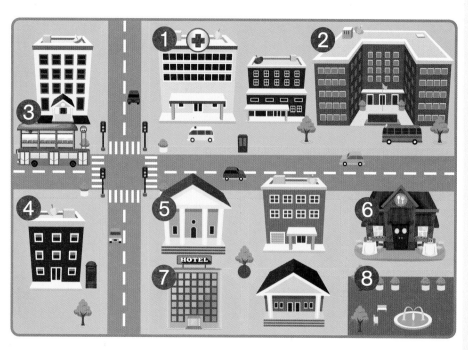

1. ho __ pit __ l

2. s __ hoo __

3. b __ s st __ p

4. p __ st off __ ce

5. m __ seu __

6. r __ sta __ ran __

7. h __ t __ __ __

8. __ a __ k

C **Busy Day**

Help them to finish their chores! Listen, number, and trace.

D Mixed Up Signs

Put the signs on the correct places. Find and write.

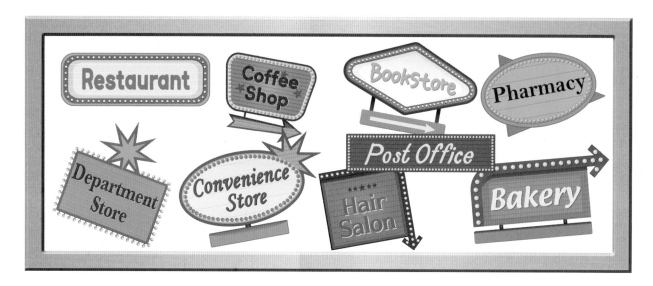

1.

2.

3.

4.

5.

6.

7.

8.

9.

They eat lunch in the cafeteria.

A School Days

Tommy and Timmy do lots of things together. Match and write the names of the places.

1.

They run in the

_____

after school.

2.

They eat lunch in the

_____.

3.

They read books in the

_____.

B Read Again!

Where do Tommy and Timmy eat lunch?

_____

2. Directions & Locations T2

A Words to Know

Highlight the words you know.

Day 3

Target Words				
north	south	east	west	left
right	straight	across	corner	here
there	in	on	under	behind
in front of	between	next to	into	out of

B Town Map

See the streets of my town. Look and write.

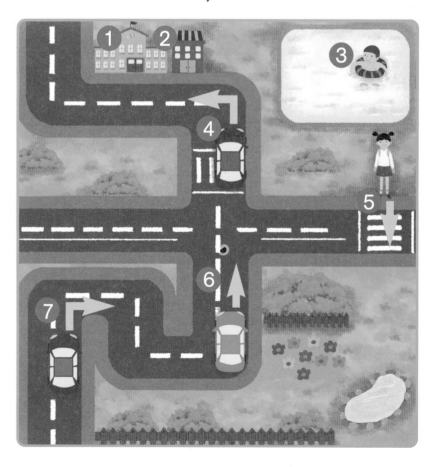

1. around the
   _ or _ er

2. n _ xt _ _
   the school

3. _ _ the pool

4. turn l _ f _

5. a _ ro _ _
   the street

6. go st _ aig _ _

7. turn r _ _ ht

C **Location Search**

Search for the items in the house. Circle and write.

1. The mirror is _____ the closet.

2. The rubber duck is _____ the bathtub.

3. The clock is _____ the wall.

4. The robot is _____ the table.

D **Odd One Out**

Find the different word. Read and circle.

1. north   south   corner   west

2. left   straight   right   in front of

3. on   here   under   in

E Tidy Up

Clean up your room. Read and number.

There are 1. a doll in the bookcase, 2. a book on the bed, 3. a bag next to the bed, and 4. a ball under the chair. Please clean up your room.

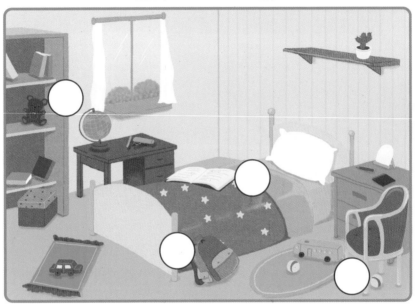

F Compass Hunt

Name the items. Look and write.

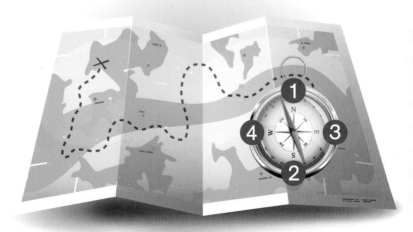

1. n _____

2. s _____

3. e _____

4. w _____

A little baby came out of the peach.

A Dangerous Adventure

Little Peachling is strong and brave. Look and choose.

1.

| a | A monster went into the peach. |
| b | A little baby came out of the peach. |

2.

| a | What is on the plate? |
| b | What is under the plate? |

3.

| a | They arrived in front of the castle. |
| b | They arrived behind the castle. |

B Write Right!

Unscramble and write.

| A little baby | the peach. | out of | came |

Review

Day 5

A Places in a Town

Find different ways to move and places to go.
Unscramble and write.

1. r n c o e r

2. r o s s a c

3. a i r g t h s t

4. g h r i t

5. f t l e

6. i n d b e h

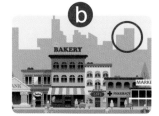

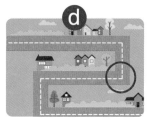

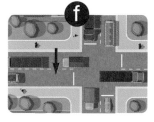

B Places to Go

See each place. Look, choose, and trace.

1.
restaurant
theater
hotel

2.
store
bank
park

C Word Search

Look at the pictures and guess the places.
Circle the words and write.

1.

_____

2.

_____

3.

_____

4.

_____

5.

_____

6.

_____

l	i	b	r	a	r	y	s	w	m	n
a	w	k	t	u	l	x	p	t	u	s
v	y	y	z	v	x	m	a	n	s	u
s	u	p	e	r	m	a	r	k	e	t
e	t	v	x	b	a	n	k	t	u	v
b	a	k	e	r	y	w	y	z	m	e

D My Town

Visit my town. Look and write.

This is my town. The bank is
1. _____ the hair salon.
The bakery is 2. _____
the hair salon and the
3. _____. The
4. _____ is next to
the supermarket.

3. Transportation

A Words to Know

Highlight the words you know.

Target Words

transportation	bicycle	bus	car
ambulance	airplane	ship	jet
helicopter	yacht	jeep	taxi
fire engine	subway	train	van
motorcycle	truck	boat	

B Transportation Means

Find different ways to move. Look and write.

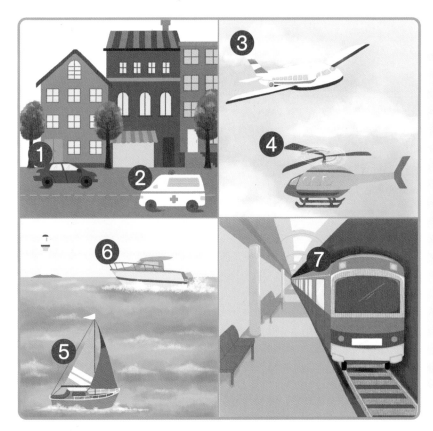

1. ca __

2. am __ ulanc __

3. a __ r __ lane

4. __ el __ copter

5. b __ a __

6. y __ c __ t

7. su __ w __ y

C Transportation Types

Choose the matching words. Look and circle.

1.

taxi

truck

motorcycle

2.

jet

taxi

jeep

3.

bus

van

ambulance

4.

airplane

bicycle

motorcycle

D On the Highway

See the words on the highway sign. Look and count.

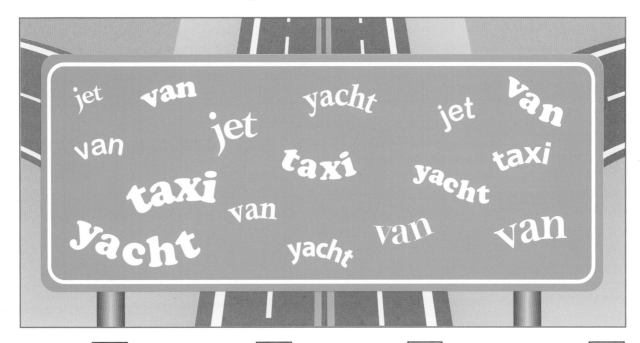

1. van ☐   2. taxi ☐   3. jet ☐   4. yacht ☐

E Transportation Shadows

See the shadow of each type of transportation. Look and write.

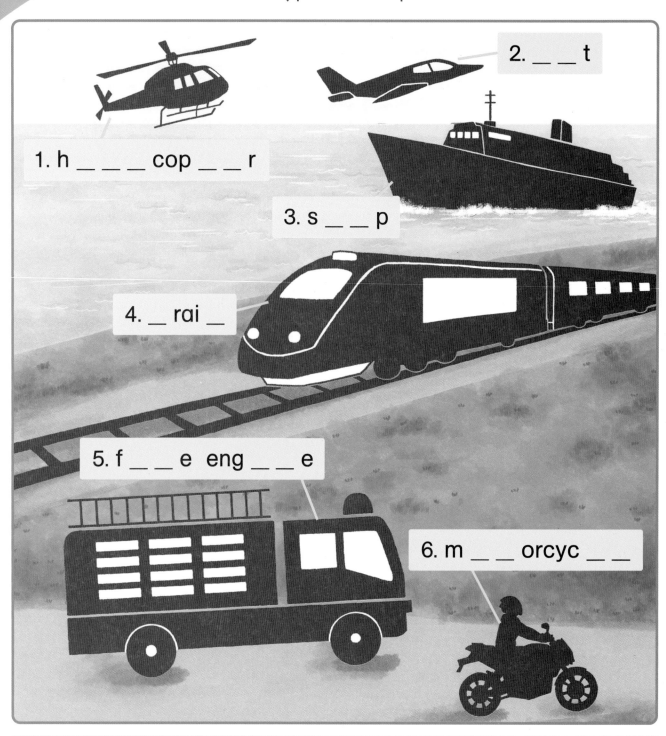

2. _ _ t

1. h _ _ _ cop _ _ r

3. s _ _ p

4. _ rai _

5. f _ _ e eng _ _ e

6. m _ _ orcyc _ _

These are types of t _ _ ans _ _ o _ _ t _ _ ti _ _ _ s!

A **A Trip to Cairo**

Carey is travelling with her parents. Read and circle the correct word.

1.

"Hurry up! The truck | taxi is waiting."

2.

Carey and her parents get on the fire engine | airplane .

3.

Carey stares out the bus | car window.

B **Write Right!**

Unscramble and write.

her parents.   takes   with   She   a taxi

4. Nature

A Words to Know

Highlight the words you know.

Target Words				
nature	cave	cloud	desert	flower
forest	grass	hill	island	lake
land	meadow	mountain	ocean	plant
pond	rock	river	sand	sea
stone	tree			

Day 3

B Island Paradise

Explore the island. Look and write.

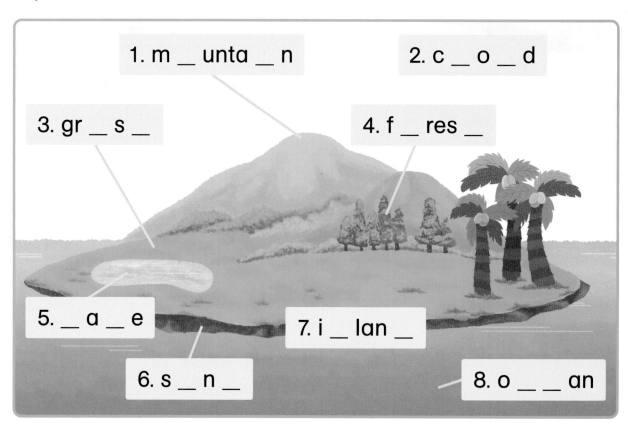

1. m _ unta _ n

2. c _ o _ d

3. gr _ s _

4. f _ res _

5. _ a _ e

6. s _ n _

7. i _ lan _

8. o _ _ an

C Nature View

See the nature. Connect and write twice.

1.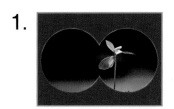

p	h	y	n	i
n	l	a	l	t

p				t
		plant		

2.

f	e	a	w	t	k
p	l	o	n	e	r

3.

n	w	a	t	o	v
m	e	u	d	l	w

D Famous Places

See the places around the world. Look, number, and trace.

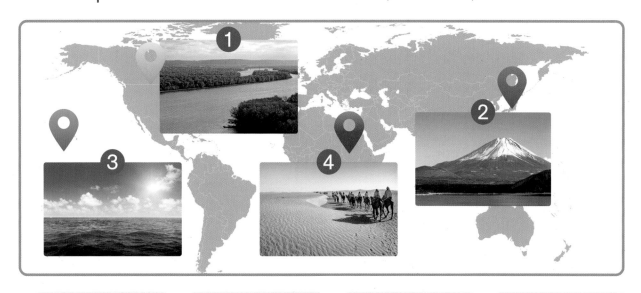

	the Mississippi **River**		the Pacific **Ocean**		**Mount** Fuji		the Sahara **Desert**

E Nature Maze

Enjoy the nature. Follow and write twice.

1. **CAVE** cave

2. **POND** pond

3. **HILL** hill

4. **ROCK** rock

5. **STONE** stone

6. **LAND** land

Day 4

There is one fruit tree.

A Desert Animals

The animals are looking for food. Find and write.

1.

   The animals travel across the _____.

2. There is one fruit _____.

3.

   The king has some _____ and plants.

Word Bank

desert   flowers   tree

B Read Again!

How many fruit trees are there?

_____

A Postcard

Complete the postcard for your friend.

POSTCARD

Hello. I am travelling Hawaii.
Here are some pictures from
my travels for you.
I saw the beautiful
1. s __ __ ,
2. f __ __ __ __ __ s, and
3. p __ __ __ __ s. See you
tomorrow.

B Angry Letters

Calm down the letters. Unscramble and write twice.

1. i b l e c y c _____ _____

2. u b w a s y _____ _____

3. u l a m b c e a n _____ _____

4. c o l i h e t e r p _____ _____

C Holiday Plan

Find their holiday plans. Look and write.

1.

I will take an _____ and go to the _____.

2.

I will take a _____ and go to the _____.

3.

I will take a _____ and go to the _____.

4.

I will ride a _____ and go to the _____.

5. Classroom & Subjects

A Words to Know

Highlight the words you know.

Target Words

classroom	textbook	math	history
P.E.	music	science	social studies
art	book bag	dictionary	scissors
paper	crayon	glue	pencil case
eraser	book	ruler	notebook
pen	desk	chair	whiteboard

Day 1

B Bag Packing

Get ready for school. Look and write.

1. pe __ __ il c __ se

2. book b __ g

3. s __ iss __ rs

4. g __ u __

5. r __ l __ __

6. t __ __ tb __ __ k

C Time Table

Complete today's school schedule. Find and write.

1 9:00 a.m.	2 10:00 a.m.	3 11:00 a.m.	4 1:00 p.m.	5 2:00 p.m.
s_____e	_____	_____	_____	_____

Word Bank

math　　P.E.　　art　　science　　social studies

D Classroom Items

Look around the classroom. Read and circle the pictures.

I see one whiteboard, two pens, three chairs, four books, six desks, and one dictionary.

E Picture to Word

Guess the word. Circle, match, and write.

1	2	3	4	5

paper _____   _____   _____   _____

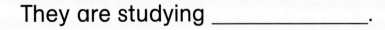

deskerasernotebookpapercrayon

F Study Time

See what they are studying. Look and write.

1.    She is studying _____.

2. They are studying _____.

3.    He is studying _____.

It's time for music class.

A John and Jane's Routine

John and Jane are having class. Look and choose.

1.

a	It's time for art class.
b	It's time for music class.
c	It's time for science class.

2.

a	It's time for P.E. class.
b	It's time for history class.
c	It's time for math class.

B Write Right!

Unscramble and write.

| time | class. | for | It's | music |

6. Months & Special Days

A Words to Know

Highlight the words you know.

Target Words

January	February	March	April	May
June	July	August	September	
October	November	December		
birthday	New Year's Day		Valentine's Day	
Halloween	Thanksgiving		Christmas	

B Picture Pairs

Look at the picture hints and write the missing letters.

1.

Val __ nt __ ne's Day
in F __ brua __ y

2.

Hall __ we ___
in O __ tob ___

3.

T __ an __ sgivi __ g
in Nov __ m __ er

4.

C __ ris __ m __ s
in De ____ ber

C Special Days

Break the code to get the letters. Find and write.

a	e	o	i	l	y	h	s	r	d

1.

b __ __ t __ __ __ __

2.

H __ __ __ __ w __ __ n

3.

T __ __ nk __ g __ v __ ng

4.

C __ __ __ __ tm __ __

These are __ pec __ __ __ __ __ __ __ __ .

D Angry Letters

Calm down the letters. Unscramble and write.

1. a n u J a r y

2. e F a r y r u b

3. p i l r A

4. r M a c h

E Picture Clues

Guess the name of each special day. Write the words.

1. _____

2. _____

3. _____

4. _____

F Busy Bee

Look at the busy bee. Write the months in order.

Day 4

A Maggie's Surprise Party

Today is Maggie's birthday. Read and write the common word.

1.

Today is Maggie's _____.
She thinks there must be a
surprise party for her.

2.

Maggie is disappointed because
they forgot her _____.

3.

Then, Maggie's friends and her
mother shout, "Happy_____,
Maggie." She is excited and happy.

B Read Again!

What day is it today?

_____

Day 5

A Math Game

Do the math to make the words. Find and write.

1.

   Change − ange + rist + mas

   = _____

2.

   bird − d + th + day

   = _____

3.

   Thanks + giv + ings − s

   = _____

B Odd One Out

Find the different word. Read and circle.

1. art — history — eraser — science

2. July — March — April — Christmas

3. paper — birthday — pen — ruler

4. June — May — science — August

C Crossword Fun

Search for the letters. Find and write.

Across

1. My family gets together on 🔔 eve.
2. The first month of the year is JAN.
3. May I use your 📏 ?
4. I have a 🎃 party.

Down

5. I don't like 📖 .
6. I have ✂️ .
7. I like to study 📖 .
8. 📐 is my favorite subject.

7. Shopping

A) Words to Know

Highlight the words you know.

Target Words

shopping	store	clothes	groceries	shoes
sale	price	cashier	customer	salesperson
gift	buy	sell	cheap	expensive
bag	cash	coin	change	credit card

B) Shopping at the Store

Look at the store pictures. Look and write.

1. c _ st _ m _ r

2. cr _ d _ t ca _ d

3. b _ g

4. s _ oe

5. _ ale _ p _ rs _ n

6. c _ ot _ es

7. s _ _ e

C Opposite Hunt

Find the opposite word pairs. Look and write.

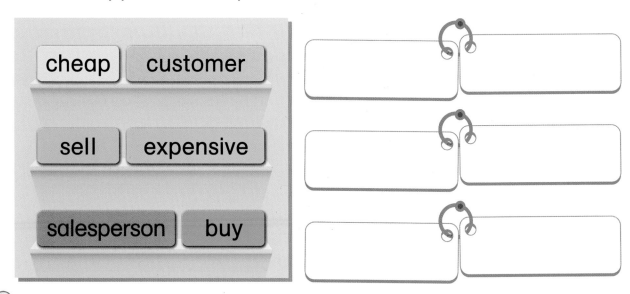

D Jumbled Shopping

Rearrange the letters. Unscramble and write in lowercase.

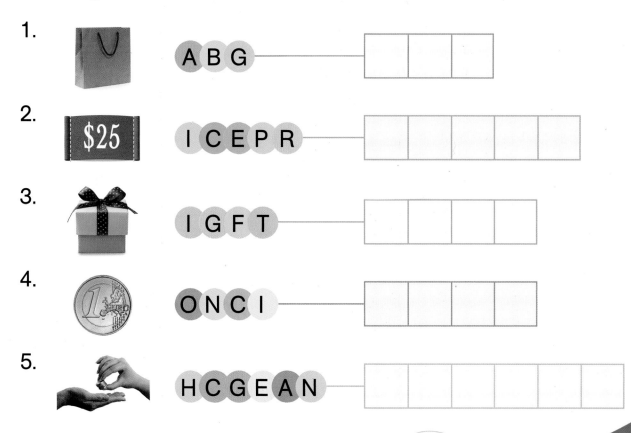

1. A B G

2. I C E P R

3. I G F T

4. O N C I

5. H C G E A N

E Scavenger Hunt

Find the differences between the two pictures. Look, circle, and write twice in alphabetical order.

groceries

cash

gift

sale

clothes

bag

price

credit card

1. _____ _____   2. _____ _____

3. _____ _____   4. _____ _____

5. _____ _____   6. _____ _____

She wants to buy a watch chain for him.

 A **First Christmas**

It is Jim and Della's first Christmas. Read and circle.

1.

Della wants to buy a nice
| gift | bag | for him.

2.

Della goes to the hair salon to
| buy | sell | her hair.

3.

Della buys an | expensive | cheap |
watch chain for Jim.

B **Write Right!**

Unscramble and write.

| for him. | She | a watch chain | wants | to buy |

8. Measurement

A. Words to Know

Highlight the words you know.

Target Words

many	much	a lot of	a few	a little
some	a bag of	a bottle of	a bowl of	a box of
a can of	a cup of	a glass of	a loaf of	a piece of
a pair of	a slice of	a spoonful of		

B. Snack Bar

Enjoy all kinds of snacks. Look and write.

1. a c _ _ of coke

2. a _ o _ t _ e of water

3. a p _ e _ e of cake

4. a _ o _ _ of bread

5. a b _ _ of chips

6. a b _ _ of chocolates

7. _ a _ _ candies

Lunch Time

Look at the pictures. Match and write.

1.
2.
3.
4.

m __ n __

a f __ w

a l __ tt __ e

m __ c __

cheese

milk

sandwiches

apples

 Yummy Dessert

Look at the scattered words. Connect and write twice.

1.

a	boxes	of	cake
four	piece		chocolate

_____

_____

2.

three	loaf	of	chips
a	bags		bread

_____

_____

3.

a	bottles	of	water
two	bowl		soup

_____

_____

E Cookie Recipe

Let's make cookies. Fill in the blank.

· Recipe ·

1. a __ lass of milk

2. a sp __ __ n __ __ __ of sugar

3. a b __ __ l of flour

4. a s __ ice of butter

5. a li __ __ le salt

F Categorizing Food

Categorize the food. Find and write.

a cup of	a bag of	a box of
tea		

He took a bowl of soup.

 A Eat, Coat, Eat

Once there was a man. He went to a party. Look and choose.

1.

a	Take a loaf of bread and go away!
b	Take a piece of bread and go away!

2.

a	He took a spoonful of soup.
b	He took a bowl of soup.

3.

a	He took a glass of juice.
b	He took a can of juice.

B Write Right!

Unscramble and write.

soup.	He	a bowl of	took

A Window Shopping

Look through the store windows. Look and circle.

1.

salesperson

cashier

customer

2.

clothes

shoes

groceries

3.

cheap

cashier

expensive

4.

gift

customer

cashier

Day 5

B Tuna Sandwich

Look at the ingredients. Match and write.

☐ some lettuce

☐ a can of tuna

☐ a slice of cheese

☐ two pieces of bread

C Shopping List

Go on a shopping trip! Read, number, and fill in the blanks.

Shopping List

1. a l_ _ _f of bread

2. a _ i _ ce of cake

3. a c_ _n of coke

4. s_ _m_ apples

5. a lit_ _l_ cheese

6. m_ _n_ bags

7. a p_ _i_ of shoes

A Needle and Thread

Sew the torn clothes. Read and match.

1. A little baby • • a taxi with her parents.

2. Today is • • for music class.

3. It's time • • came out of the peach.

4. She takes • • Maggie's birthday.

B Back on Track

Look at the train off the track. Unscramble and write.

1. eat | They | lunch | in the cafeteria.

_____

2. is | There | tree. | one | fruit

_____

3. wants | She | to buy | for him. | a watch chain

_____

Day 5

C My Hometown

See the view of my hometown. Find and write. Then rewrite the sentences.

1. She wants to _____ a watch chain for him.

   _____

2. They eat lunch in the _____.

   _____

3. He took _____ soup.

   _____

4. It's time for _____ class.

   _____

5. There is one fruit _____.

   _____

Word Bank

| tree | a bowl of | buy | cafeteria | music |

1. Places

p.2
B 1. hospital 2. school 3. bus stop
4. post office 5. museum
6. restaurant 7. hotel 8. park

p.3
C 1. bakery 2. supermarket 3. bank
4. pharmacy 5. library 6. post office
7. cafeteria 8. hair salon

p.4
D 1. pharmacy 2. department store
3. post office 4. hair salon
5. bookstore 6. coffee shop
7. restaurant
8. convenience store 9. bakery

p.5
A 1. They eat lunch in the cafeteria.
2. They read books in the library.
3. They run in the playground after school.
B They eat lunch in the cafeteria.

2. Directions & Locations

p.6
B 1. corner 2. next to 3. in 4. left
5. across 6. straight 7. right

p.7
C 1. next to 2. in 3. on 4. under

D 1. corner 2. in front of 3. here

p.8
F

F 1. north 2. south 3. east 4. west

p.9
A 1. b 2. a 3. a
B A little baby came out of the peach.

Review(1, 2)

p.10
A 1. corner, ⓓ 2. across, ⓕ
3. straight, ⓔ 4. right, ⓒ 5. left, ⓐ
6. behind, ⓑ
B 1. theater 2. park

p.11
C 1. bakery 2. bank 3. museum
4. library 5. supermarket 6. park
D 1. next to 2. between 3. coffee shop 4. pharmacy

3. Transportation

p.12
B 1. car 2. ambulance 3. airplane
4. helicopter 5. boat 6. yacht
7. subway

p.13
C 1. truck 2. jeep 3. bus 4. bicycle
D 1. 6 2. 3 3. 3 4. 4

p.14
F 1. helicopter 2. jet 3. ship 4. train
5. fire engine 6. motorcycle / transportations

p.15
A 1. taxi 2. airplane 3. car
B She takes a taxi with her parents.

4. Nature

p.16
B 1. mountain 2. cloud 3. grass
4. forest 5. lake 6. sand 7. island
8. ocean

p.17
C 1. plant 2. flower 3. meadow
D 1. the Mississippi River 2. Mount Fuji 3. the Pacific Ocean 4. the Sahara Desert

p.18
F 1. cave 2. rock 3. land 4. hill
5. pond 6. stone

p.19
A 1. desert 2. tree 3. flowers
B There is one fruit tree.

Review(3, 4)

p.20
A 1. sea 2. flowers 3. plants
B 1. bicycle 2. subway
3. ambulance 4. helicopter

p.21
C 1 airplane, desert 2. ship, island
3. train, river 4. bicycle, forest

5. Classroom & Subjects

p.22
B 1. pencil case 2. book bag
3. scissors 4. glue 5. ruler 6. textbook

p.23
C 1. science 2. art 3. math 4. P.E.
5. social studies
D

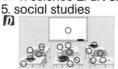

p.24
F 1. paper 2. eraser 3. notebook
4. crayon 5. desk
F 1. math 2. P.E. 3. science

p.25
A 1. b 2. a
B It's time for music class.

6. Months & Special Days

p.26
B 1. Valentine's Day in February
2. Halloween in October
3. Thanksgiving in November
4. Christmas in December

p.27
C 1. birthday 2. Halloween
3. Thanksgiving 4. Christmas / special days
D 1. January 2. February 3. April
4. March

p.28
F 1. Christmas 2. birthday
3. Halloween 4. New Year's Day
F May-June-July-August-September-October-November-December

p.29
A 1~3. birthday
B Today is Maggie's birthday.

Review(5, 6)

p.30
A 1. Christmas 2. birthday
3. Thanksgiving

B 1. eraser 2. Christmas 3. birthday
4. science

p.31
C 1. Christmas 2. January 3. ruler
4. Halloween 5. history 6. scissors
7. science 8. math

7. Shopping

p.32
B 1. customer 2. credit card 3. bag
4. shoe 5. salesperson 6. clothes 7. sale

p.33
C cheap-expensive / customer-salesperson / sell-buy
D 1. bag 2. price 3. gift 4. coin 5. change

p.34
F 1. bag 2. cash 3. clothes
4. groceries 5. price 6. sale

p.35
A 1. gift 2. sell 3. expensive
B She wants to buy a watch chain for him.

8. Measurement

p.36
B 1. can 2. bottle 3. piece 4. loaf
5. bag 6. box 7. many

p.37
C 1. some apples 2. many sandwiches 3. a little cheese
4. much milk
D 1. a piece of cake 2. a loaf of bread 3. a bowl of soup

p.38
F 1. glass 2. spoonful 3. bowl
4. slice 5. little
F a cup of : tea, coffee / a bag of: chips, groceries / a box of: donuts, chocolates

p.39
A 1. a 2. b 3. a
B He took a bowl of soup.

Review(7, 8)

p.40
A 1. customer 2. shoes 3. cheap
4. cashier
B ①-some lettuce, ②-two pieces of bread, ③-a can of tuna, ④-a slice of cheese

p.41
C 1. a loaf of bread 2. a slice of cake 3. a can of coke 4. some apples 5. a little cheese
6. many bags 7. a pair of shoes

Expressions Review

p.42
A 1. A little baby came out of the peach. 2. Today is Maggie's birthday. 3. It's time for music class.
4. She takes a taxi with her parents.
B 1. They eat lunch in the cafeteria.
2. There is one fruit tree. 3. She wants to buy a watch chain for him.

p.43
C 1. buy 2. cafeteria 3. a bowl of
4. music 5. tree

Places

bookstore

Places

department store

Places

hospital

Places

hotel

Places

library

Places

museum

Places

post office

Places

playground

Places

supermarket

Places

theater

Places

restaurant

Places

amusement park

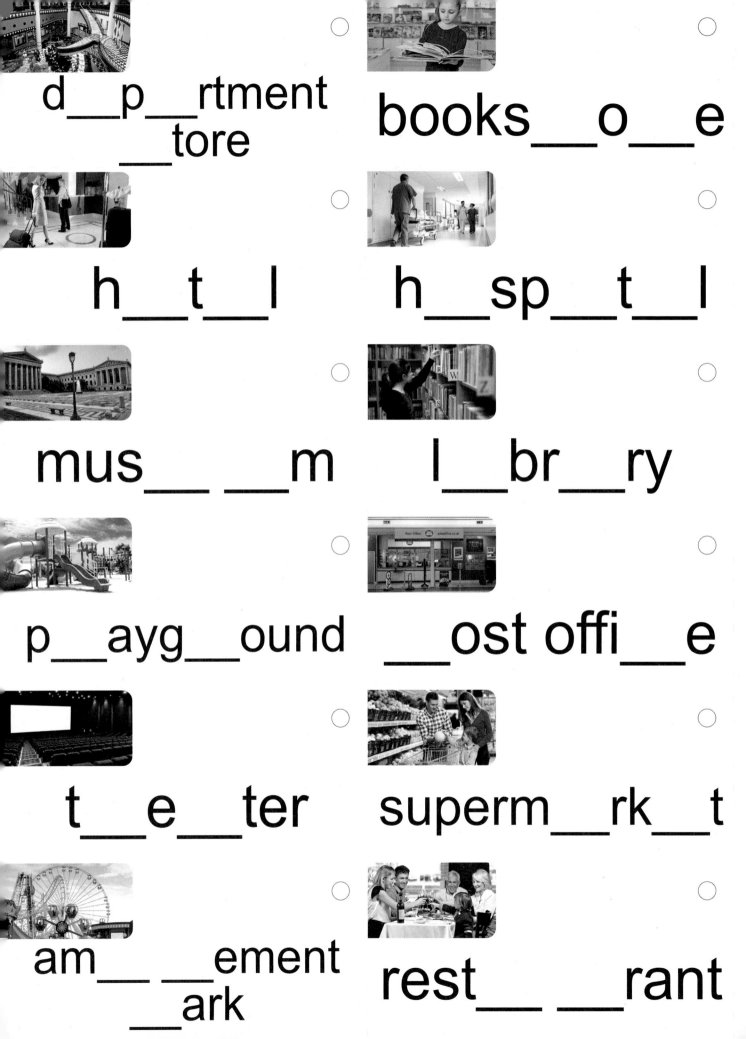

d__p__rtment __tore

books__o__e

h__t__l

h__sp__t__l

mus__ __m

l__br__ry

p__ayg__ound

__ost offi__e

t__e__ter

superm__rk__t

am__ __ement __ark

rest__ __rant

left

right

east

west

south

north

straight

corner

in front of

behind

next to

between

ri__ __t   le__t

w__st   e__st

nor__ __   sou__ __

c__rn__r   str__ __ght

b__h__nd   in __r__nt of

betw__ __n   n__xt __o

transportation

airplane

bicycle

helicopter

subway

train

yacht

motorcycle

fire engine

van

taxi

ambulance

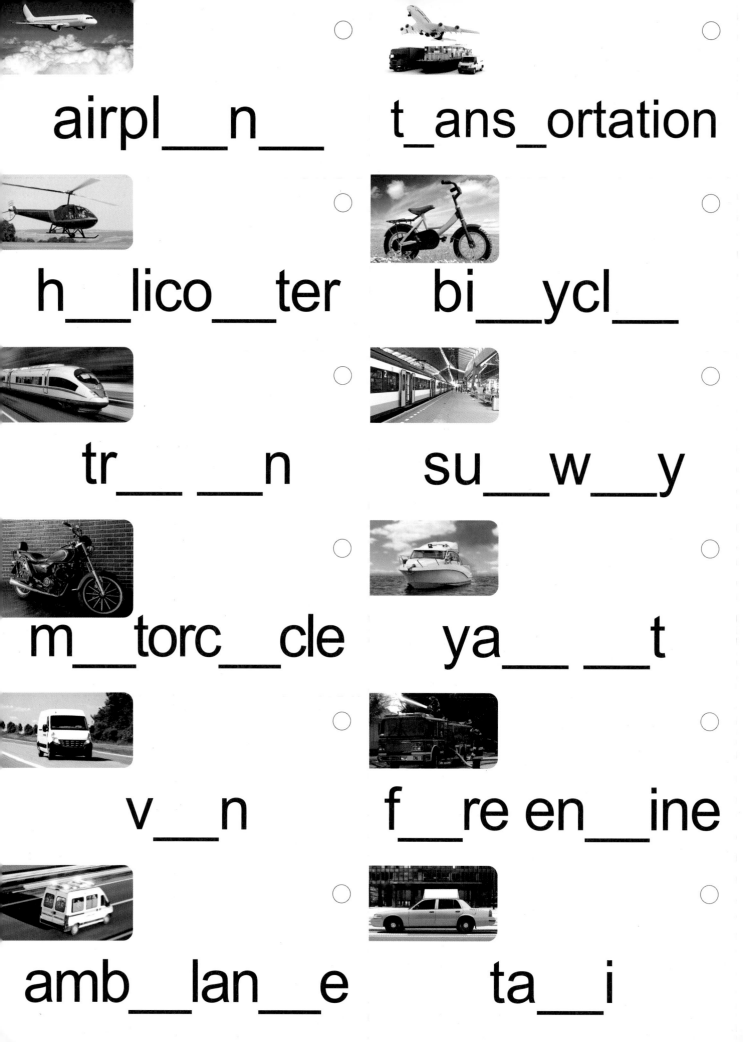

airpl__n__   t_ans_ortation

h__lico__ter   bi__ycl__

tr__ __n   su__w__y

m__torc__cle   ya__ __t

v__n   f__re en__ine

amb__lan__e   ta__i

nature

cave

forest

grass

mountain

lake

land

plant

pond

island

desert

ocean

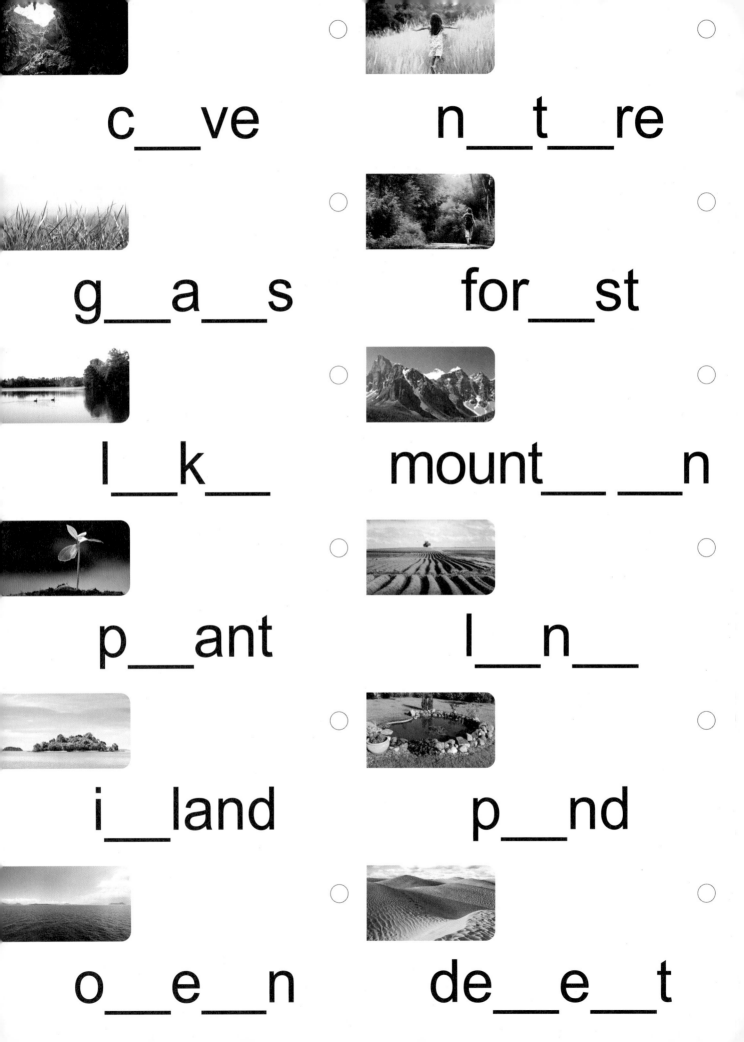

c__ve   n__t__re

g__a__s   for__st

l__k__   mount____n

p__ant   l__n__

i__land   p__nd

o__e__n   de__e__t

book bag

eraser

crayon

dictionary

notebook

pencil case

ruler

scissors

math

science

history

social studies

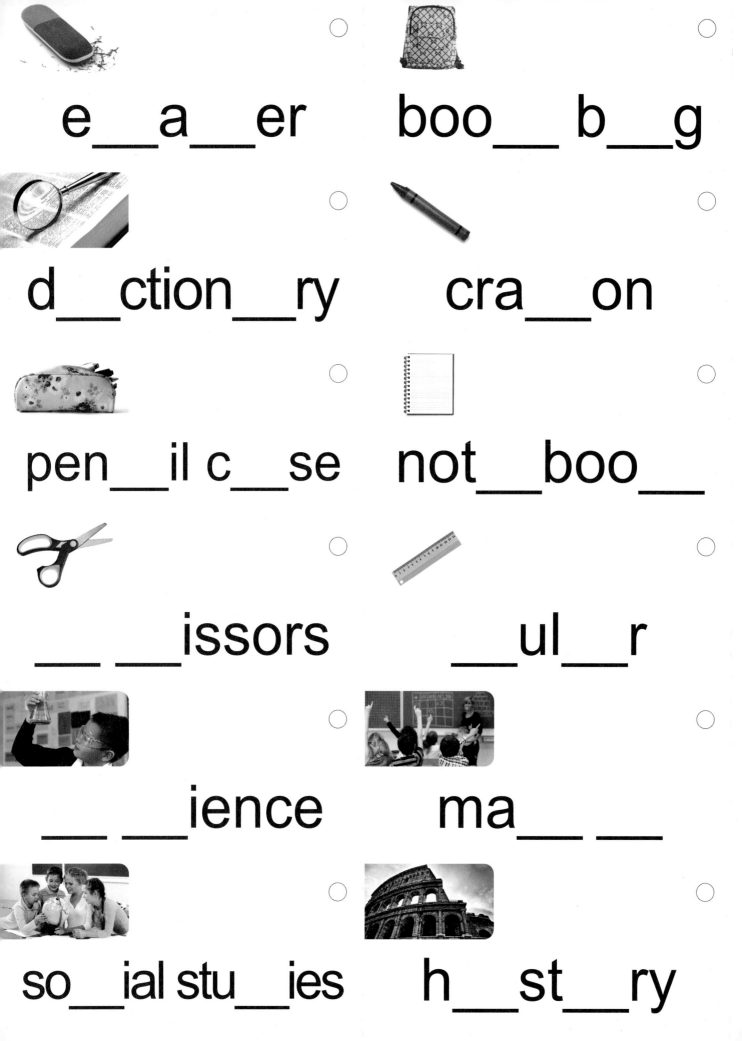

e__a__er

boo__ b__g

d__ction__ry

cra__on

pen__il c__se

not__boo__

__ __issors

__ul__r

__ __ience

ma__ __

so__ial stu__ies

h__st__ry

January

February

March

May

July

September

November

December

Christmas

Halloween

Thanksgiving

birthday

Fe____uary J___n___ary

M___y Mar___ ___

Se___t___mber J___ ___y

De___em___er No___em___er

Hall___w___n Chri___ ___mas

bir___ ___day Th___nk___giving

Shopping

credit card

Shopping

sale

Shopping

gift

Shopping

price

Shopping

clothes

Shopping

groceries

Shopping

expensive

Shopping

salesperson

Shopping

customer

Shopping

cheap

Shopping

shopping

Shopping

store

s__le

cr__d__t c__rd

pr__ __e

gi__t

gro__er__es

clo__ __es

s__les__erson

exp__ns__ve

ch__ __p

c__st__mer

s__ore

sho__ __ing

many

much

a cup of

a piece of

a glass of

a bottle of

a bowl of

a pair of

a lot of

a bag of

a loaf of

a slice of

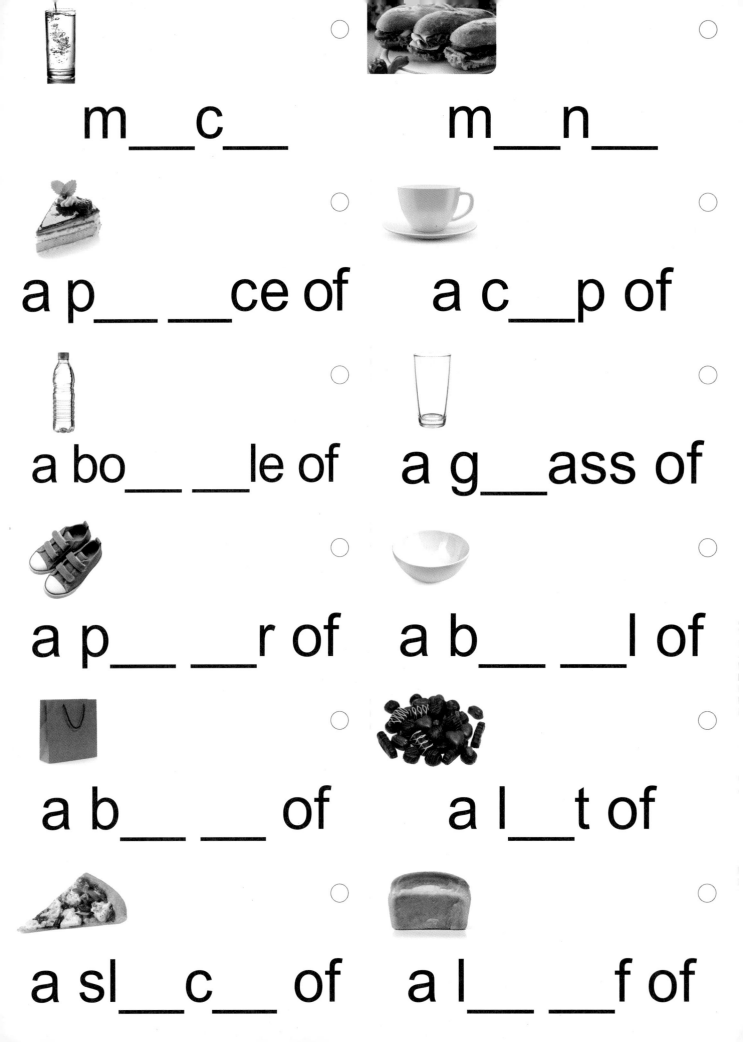

m__c__

m__n__

a p_____ce of

a c___p of

a bo_____le of

a g___ass of

a p_____r of

a b_____l of

a b_____ of

a l__t of

a sl__c____ of

a l_____f of